# When Angels Dream
## And other things

Poetic Works for the New Millennium

By Michael Romo

Copyright © 2007 by Michael Romo

First edition

Published by Michael Romo through lulu.com

For info about reproducing contact Michael Romo at 6680 Navarette Ave. Atascadero Calif.93422 or micromo66.com or 805-610-1153

Id: 839159

ISBN: 978-0-6151-5012-3

# Table of contents

**Preface** — 7

**Introduction** — 9

**Poetry** — 15

| | |
|---|---|
| Eden | 17 |
| God | 19 |
| Judgment day | 20 |
| Life | 23 |
| Lisa's Smile | 25 |
| Truth | 27 |
| The Bells of Hell | 29 |
| Magick | 31 |
| Color | 33 |
| Marie Antoinette | 35 |
| Obsession | 36 |
| Schizophrenia | 38 |
| San Francisco Lady | 41 |
| An Angel's Kiss | 43 |
| The Genie | 45 |
| Freedom | 47 |
| Vampires | 49 |
| I Am | 50 |

| | |
|---|---|
| I Am the Lizard King | 51 |
| Romo | 53 |
| Prose a Rose | 54 |
| Disneyland | 55 |
| Sunshine | 56 |
| Thoughts | 57 |
| The Reapers Wisdom | 59 |
| The Tombstone Lament | 61 |
| Poppies | 65 |
| California | 66 |
| Memories | 68 |
| Sweets | 69 |
| Generation X | 71 |
| Generation X revisited | 72 |
| Death | 75 |
| Maynard | 77 |
| Treasure | 81 |
| Fateful fantasy | 82 |
| When Angels Dream | 83 |
| **Finis** | 85 |
| **Suggested reading** | 86 |
| **Notes** | 89 |
| **Art Credits** | 90 |

# Preface

My prose is ponderous
My poetry is simple
I live in the land of the lost
Because I loved her dimple

Cover drawing by
**Katerina Koukiotis**
Copyright and all rights reserved
http://members.aol.com/katerinaart/katerinaart.html/welcomepage.html

With drawings inside by
**Michelle Romo**
Copyright and all rights reserved

And by **Myself**
See **art credits** page 90

# Introduction:

If a book was written about my life it would probably be found in the fiction part of the bookstore. My life has been a bizarre collage of strange occurrences. As a child I wanted to grow up to be either a beatnik or a superhero. I always felt different, but somehow the same. I have a chameleon like ability to blend in with whatever group I am around. Because of this my life experience has been extraordinarily enriched with odd combinations of cultural attachments. Add to this seven years working at Atascadero state hospital for the criminally insane and you get some idea where the schizophrenic aspects of my poetry (and writing) come from. I was often reminded of what Ken Kesey must have gone through before he wrote "One Flew over the Cuckoos Nest".

Naturally, if left to my own, my art is dark. But since I have been writing poetry on "poetry.com" I have been trying to concentrate on being more positive in what I was trying to say. Perhaps at times it has become saccharine. I hope at least it remains entertaining.

My artistic influences are so numerous it is almost impossible to distill to one source. Perhaps being a product of the television media generation is most obvious. I think when I have quoted others it should be obvious, but one of my greatest fears is accidentally plagiarizing someone else's work. If such were the case I would have no problem acknowledging my debt to the others' works. We are a product of our environment, and this has to have an effect.

Computers and the internet have made people very aware of copyrights and I believe this hurts art, a friend of mine once said "if someone stole one of my songs I'd write another one". I think it is not stealing to like someone's work so much that you would like to see or hear it before buying, not all of us are rich, but if you try to get rich by taking, this is immoral. God will deal with these problems.

In our modern economy, letting people try it first is the best advertising you can buy it promotes word of mouth advertising that is impossible by any other means.

The chance for us to all to have our fifteen minutes is greater than it ever was. I would love to make money from it, but I'm really a people person and just knowing I am being read would be the greatest thrill.

I started writing poetry at about age 11. I was heavily influenced by the poetic works of songwriters, English poets especially Samuel Taylor Coleridge, and American poets especially Poe. I have had a lot of education (perhaps too much), and always took my education seriously. I was always glad that I got whatever grades I got, honestly.

I look at the bible as a history and philosophy book. It is fascinating when you become aware of the truth of the stories there. I have studied every major religion and the occult to get an objective viewpoint. Often though, it surprises my friends, when I let them know that I am a Christian. I am irreverent and not dogmatic. And not one of those hypocrite Christians that I know Jesus would have hated. I think of Jesus as a rebel that perfectly worshipped a god that he thought was greater than him and believed in him so much that he was even willing to die because he truly believed that god would save him. On the other hand though I often say Satan does his best work in church.

I was drawn to poetry as a way of telling a story. I wrote many poems in many different styles, but since at that time I wanted to be a musician, I wrote in pretty strict meter. It has been hard for me to break out of that mold. But my goal here was to write poetry and not songs.

Not rhyming was very difficult. I have always felt a need for my rhyming to not be banal and not rhyming is the greatest freedom from that curse. I have read a little of Ginsberg but I am holding off reading him until I take a break in my writing because I do not want to be too heavily influenced.

I heard Mick Jagger on TV. saying he wrote in prose I said to myself" no way" he is a great poet. I'm not going to argue with Mick but I still think he is a great poet. He is a master at the craft of telling a story or saying whatever he wants well.

Morrison's book of poetry was really good. At the time, I think, familiarity bred contempt, but his work seems to hold up to me. Musically he was very uneven, but I am always impressed in the movie (the original) where he gets off of the plane and when he is asked his profession he says "poet". This really impressed upon me that poetry was still a viable medium in this day and age. Maybe the medium is the message.

I somewhat belabor this point because there is some really great poetry fobbed off as song and people that listen to music do not want to read poetry. I took an art appreciation class years ago and truly learned to appreciate all types of art and all different styles. There is beauty everywhere.

Often artists are not appreciated until they are dead. That is a shame because an artist does what he does for a greater reason than just surviving. Possibly, he or she might do it to give greater meaning to all of our existence.

Of course, when it comes to classics, and of all time, Shakespeare is "the King". Years later the things he wrote still come back to me. I especially liked his early funny work. That was a Woody Allen reference, by the way, I'm pretty sure Woody is intelligent enough to laugh at that statement and not try to sue me for plagiarism. Like I said, we are a product of our environment. Art does not stay in boundaries well, so we should all, like what we like, not try to be too judgmental and not try to hurt anyone. O.K, I am actually asking for you to be nice about my poetry. Just in case you don't like it.

I write poetry using words like a paintbrush. Nothing is sacred and editing becomes a means to an end result which should always be more powerful than the sum of its parts. This became an immediate problem when I found I had to cut every poem to twenty lines. In the process of making it fit often times the poetry took on a completely new meaning. This was not a bad thing. This is fun for me because it's like getting to read someone else's poetry. I kind of write then decide what it means then change it to fit.

I love to read. I try to read myself critically every day to see if it is truly interesting. I read my poetry with a critical approach, looking for flaws that I can repair. But I always remember rules are meant to be broken. I think at these moments I remember e.e. cummings work. His work was intentionally written to break the rules when he wanted too. He probably opened the door to looser styled poetry which seems to be "the thing" today.

They say you should never judge a work of art until it is done, but the artists' most grave responsibility is to know when he (or she) has finished. I have a painting that I did almost 40 years ago that won a blue ribbon at the fair that I still do not feel is finished.

Very little of what I write is accidental although sometimes the inspiration is almost like throwing a puzzle together. If I were starting a religion I might even say it was inspired I however do not believe in manipulating people so I am always totally willing to disclose my secrets to anyone that wants to learn. (My god, I sound as if I was already famous, what an ego!). I think I have to believe in myself before anyone else will.

I am writing this with the assumption that my writing is entertaining, at least, because you the reader are reading this. Otherwise there would be no point in me writing. I have always felt my writing had a universal meaning (that someone would understand someday). I write in universal symbolism. But alas, there is the rub. My symbolism might not be exactly the same as another's understanding of these things. I am probably controversial at times, but, I know no sacred cows and therefore I do not seek to offend (perhaps that statement is offensive). Most of all I hope my poetry is fun. My vision is almost always clear but my vision of other people's vision is not.

I try to be objective about my work but ultimately you the reader must decide. I think the ultimate honor would be for college students to think what I have written is "cool", because that is when these things impressed me the most. God bless, Hari Krishna, and praise Allah.

Thank You

Michael Romo

P.S. I have tied real hard not to re-edit this introduction because as William Burroughs said through one of his characters "to edit is to lie". Some how the book got to be a little darker than I had originally intended, or maybe it was the influence of My Space. I dunno.

# Poetry

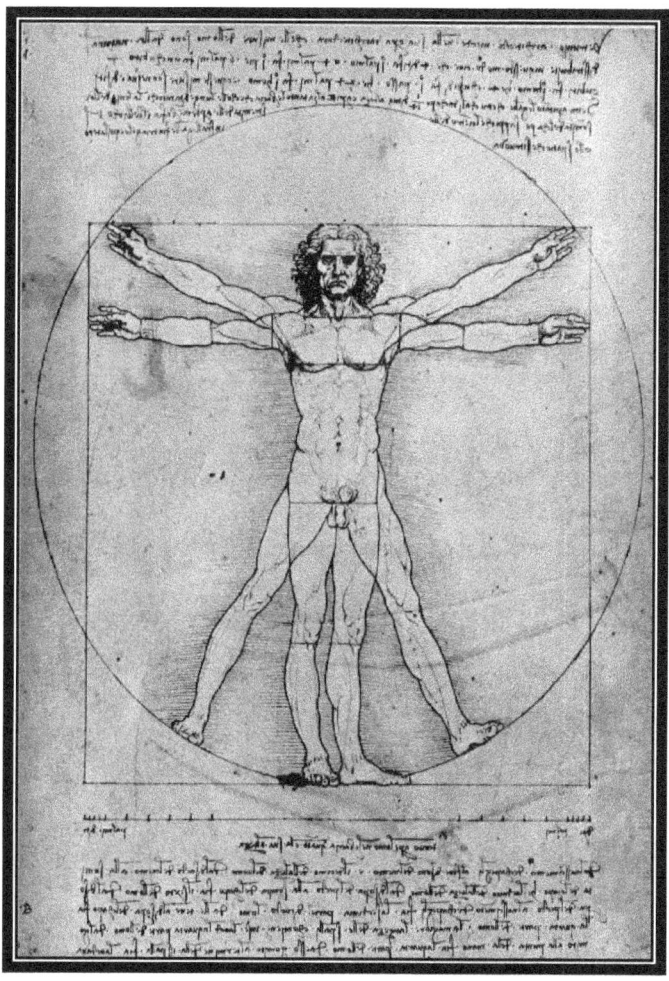

Eclectic Selections

## *Eden*

As I sit in the Garden of Eden
A place just north of Iraq
Two angels around the rivers go round
No mortal touches the sacred ground

Three dreams of things in ancient times
Four mermaids beckon to lives of crime
Such sweet smiles and pleasant voices
The hands that beckon to make bad choices

But things are fine in Eden time
Such velvet cloth to clothe us fine
And here's the answer to seal our fate
Pomegranates here, so procrastinate

Never touch what you find in the center
Or you will know the pain
Of a word that we call Sinner

# God

I asked myself once Is there a god?

I had to answer Yes

Its seems so reassuring

To know there is an omnipresent being

That knows my trials and tribulations

Perhaps he has a wonderful new world in store for us

It has been said god[3] is the opiate of the masses

Is opium power and power money?

These are questions of this world

Unbefitting an omnipresent being

I believe in God because it is easier

Than it is to not believe

And that seems to be

A good enough reason

3 pg 84

# Judgment Day

Judge not the grieving widow
Judge not the fatherless son
For God's reaction
To your cruel action
He'll see your day is done

With selfless worth
The bibles verse will be your curse
For all your evil deeds…..

Please heed that God has warned you
Throughout his fiery reign
To heed this subject mightily
Decrease the widow's pain

Never turn a deafened ear
Till the widows son is done
For his true words are sweet and just
For feeding everyone

Fear to judge the widow

And fear the widow's son

Is there no relief for the widow's son?

Until his days are done

# Life

I was born on the day of the dead
With trials of mercy burning in my head

Burn your bibles if they offend thee
Lose your troubles before you pull your eyes out
Leave your troubles down in Hades
Don't believe it before they let the Hounds out

See the sick things in the lost asylum
They know the right things
These are things we all find out

Webs of mercy webs of fire
Webs of innocence and Webs that we admire
We seek truth in the distant quagmire
Intensely giving until these things do tire

We love pestilence we love our things intense
We are all we are, because we are anarchy

Anarchy is not our life
Anarchy is done in strife
It is the only thing there is
In a world with no solution

Solutions are dissolved in water
Water is the fact of life
Life that wants, life that hungers
Trials of fire trials of ice
Things that send my spirit under

Wings of mercy wings of death
Come to Spiritize my breath
Breathe and breathe and breathe god's breath
If friends are evil that you've chosen
Go to hell and take them with you

Did I choose or did I get
Or was it chosen in a fit
Life is all these things and more
As we open up the door

# Lisa's Smile

## (Demons in the Mist)

Sweet summer love that never ends
Fans the fire of heavenly friends
Fast frenzied passion on which life depends
Soft sullen glow to light the end

The end of romance the end of pain
The start of melodies that spring again
The flowering glances that light the dark
The eyes enchanting the heart so stark

*The vampires kiss is never felt*
*But vampire dreams are like a belt*
*That wraps around the heart so pure*
*And makes it seem like a heavenly cure*

For aches and pains of loves desire
Of wood and flint to light the fire
And soft winds blow to fan the passion
That Cupid's bow will firmly fasten

Teeth that touch the neck so fair
Fingers touch the golden hair
Eyes that seize the heart and soul
Green as emeralds to pay the toll

Breath pulls in words flow out
Like silken streams of heavens spout
Music of angels that may descend
On hearts that shine in love again

Fairies on toadstools that dance for joy
Soften the sadness of their employ
Summers sweet madness will never end
But how will the sadness ever mend

Your smile is fine like wine in time
A bottle of innocence without a crime
A feast on which we never cry
That have a heart that cares to fly

# Truth

Truth is the food of the gods
Lies are only good for the death of the soul

Time is more precious than gold
The past and the future are illusions for sorrow

Love is the reason we want to live
Hate is only useful for dictators and fools

Happiness makes time fly like an eagle
Sadness makes time linger like a buzzard

Reason gives order and meaning to all things
To be stubborn gives birth to chaos and unrest

Trust is our greatest attachment to all life
Slander gives rise to being truly alone

Everything we do is a choice
Everything we do should be
Chosen wisely

# The Bells of Hell

The sons of the earth though they live by the gun

Say you got to give or it's just no Fun

You tell them once you tell them twice

But if you tell them thrice they're going to end your life

Sweet mother Jesus lost in a sweatshop

When will we all be saved when will the pain stop

Maybe I'm crazy although I think I'm not

Don't want the sun to shine on my grave plot

Who wants the bells of hell to find their paradise?

Start to sense the smell of cold peering eyes

The shroud that covers you will never see you through

You lost your innocence on things that will not do

One for the master one for the church

They skirt disaster like crows on their perch

The smile of Sardonicus is hard on our hearts
The words of the pessimist might fry all our tarts

No evil will escape us no smoke in the clouds
Forever on the lost bus lost in the crowd
Hellfire will consume itself in the stinking lie
I hope to presume my life just before I die

Presumption is dangerous presumptuously cold
No train will stop for us while still our life we hold
The dragon lives on anger the unicorn is sick
We fight for the danger of poison on a stick

The taste of the poison lies heavy on our soul
And we will be in prison when
The Bells of Hell they toll

## *Magick*

Oh sweet mysteries of life
We seldom see the underbelly of the beast
The magick moments dawns
And shows us sweet surprise
Dancing fairies rippling through
The fanciful forest of eyes delight
Prancing puzzlement through
Shimmering castles of dazzling light
These things our eyes imagine
Both dark and light
Bring magick to our minds
Once more I see the dream
I dream of heavenly virtue
We share with ethereal creatures
That fills our imagination
Bring me these things
To fill my dreams with
These magickal things I need
When I rise
So that forever we will be
At home in our hearts

And our minds will seem

To be never apart

# Color

My eyes can see in all colors
And there is not enough difference
In the colors of man
For me to say
Which is better by color?

If there were blue men and green men
I'm sure, that would stand out
But soon I'd get used to that
And I would
No longer see them as different

How shade conscious would a man have to be
To say, this color is better than that
For all colors I see
Are very pretty
And I'd have to pull one out of a hat

# Marie Antoinette

Marie Antoinette
Did a pirouette
While gathering flowers on Sunday
She said let them eat cake
Quite a mistake
Fatal words for a lady
Did she not know?
That hunger would grow
Til she was educated at the guillotine
She said I did not say that
As she sat and chat
With her servants gathered around her
Had she shared her cake
Her second mistake
She possibly could have lived longer
Did we learn the lesson of
Marie Antoinette?
Or did we forget?

# Obsession

Obsession is confession
Start to see the light
Anxiety is all you see
Every day and night

Perhaps you'll feel
When you appeal
To every open thought
The things you see
Might soon be free
Of all the things
You're taught

An open book
Will give the look
Of freedom to aspire
And love will start
To mend the heart
Of passions burning fire

There is no I in team
There is no can in but
These things were told
Grow awful cold
Just like an open cut

Obsession is confession

## Schizophrenia

Bleuler wasn't foolin
when he architected the ruin
of the dementia
we call schizophrenia

Ambivalence is no offense
Simple things seem very tense
to not know what we think is best
Putting all thought to the test

Association is invitation
to think things lost or maybe crossed
in a tangled fence that makes no sense
words that privately seem intense

Autism is a schism from,
 the warmth of human touch
you truly want to be alone
you want it oh so much

Affect is not very clear
sometimes face is made of stone
then laughter replaces crying
laughing when your heart is dying

They cant feel pain they'd feel again
this thing called joy will leave no stain
each second is a millennia
in this curse called schizophrenia

## San Francisco lady

She was a San Francisco lady
Made me purple hazy
Met her on the Haight Street
She had a real nice Ashbury
Working in a sandwich shop
Really made my heart stop
I sat and watched the hippies shop
Really made my mind stop
What a beautiful moon she had
Her sweet delicious truffles
More than a man could bear
Her sweet Alabama smile
Made me dream awhile

# An Angel's Kiss

An angel's kiss is all it seems
A breath of air A touch of spring
A gift from god is what it seems
A touch of love Of magic dreams

An angel's love is crystal clear
The purest dove That will appear
To lonely hearts that cast a tear
The angel's heart The only cure

A shooting star that won't come down
From heavens grace with jewel in crown
The purest light the peaceful dark
The tree that bends Without a mark

The angel's kiss brings all these things
I've touched this truth I've touched the wings
Words of grace from lips so sweet
Makes common love seem Bittersweet

Her every wish you will apply
For her warm love Will never die
An angel's kiss is all it seems
I know to me It's everything

# The Genie

Be careful what you ask for
Be careful who you know
I've wished I'd wished for just one wish
To set the genie free
She's beautiful she's suitable
She's quite a sight to see
With sincere eyes and sincere smile
Like legends I've been told
She'll steer our course if were not coarse
In wishes we have made
I thought I knew this genie
I thought she was my friend
Her home that was a prison
Was quite a palace divine
That sacred cell of cruel intent
Was her most treasure fine
A thousand years ago
She lived quite happily
I set her free is she still free
Without the things she loved
I hope today I've saved her day
I set the genie free

# Freedom

I saw a lovely lady
which I saved alone from three
A lady who could be my queen

I saw a lovely stretch of sea
Which should certainly be my own
I care for things that should not be
And the freedom to call these things my own

Never call the cleft desire
Which draws us to our perilous peak
For these strange creatures called desire
Will certainly draw us to our doom

Fresh lovely innocence
Treat these things as May they be
Never treat these things as pestilence
Or never shall we be called free

# Vampires

Dracula is not my friend
Even if we drink the green fairy together
Wormwood and mint and anise so sweet
Too often I've known the company of wolves
Those clever creatures that worry my waking hours
Sliding through the shadows while I think
But vampires most of all cannot be trusted
They smile and charm everyone they meet
The smell of rotten blood on their breath
They feign friendship to get what they want
With only one goal in their cold black hearts

When I meet him I tell him to go away
There is nothing for him to feed on here
No coffins, no bats, no easily amazed women
To mesmerize with your charms and promises
I say go away, wretched prince, back to your master
Lift your slight veil of mortality and give birth
To your death

 Then, shall you know peace
Only then, when your sins are cold cinders
Perhaps you shall be redeemed

# I Am

I'm an actor, a lover, an artist and a musician
I'm a father, a mother, a gypsy and a physician
I live in the minds of, all the people that I know
Perhaps I think of, places I don't know
I live in a jungle, a city, a castle
A place called Shangri La, where people, never grow old
I live on an island, with everybody naked
And everyone loves who, everyone is
Everyone is special, everyone is perfect
Everyone is someone that, I want to know
Perhaps I'm a dreamer, with Renaissance fever
Maybe I'm a genius, but so are you
Utopia is my homeland, my house, and an island
Filled with all the fruits of, the people I know
Maybe I'm crazy, perhaps I am lazy
Maybe everyone should be, just like me
If you could have, everything you wanted
Wouldn't you have, all the things that I see
I think that you would because, I am
**You**

# I am the Lizard King

*To J. Morrison*

I am the lizard king, I can do anything
I've heard the morning sing, I am a human being
I sleep in dungeons deep, where others cannot creep
My treasures in a heap, that no one else can keep

My skin grows awful cold, like bones in days of old
Some think they smell the mold, I think that, I've been sold
I sit in clothes of thread, but now I might be dead
But soon I'll clear my head, and rise up from my bed

The flames will rise, up once again, and cleanse the world of sin
And bring, what once has been, to crush their house of tin
My might shall be revealed, and all shall soon be healed
The rich will know the feel, their rule will be repealed

The kings of earth shall fall, the mighty shall all be small
No one shall hear their call when they cry to the All
The meek shall know no fear, not one left living here
With kingdoms of their own and riches they have sown

I can do anything, I am the Lizard King

# Romo

If Romo means to cast a spear
We are here We do not fear
No Rhomboid nose for all that prose
And poetry like scented rose
A challenge comes and here we go
Some think the breath of God we know
Some think we should all be low
Some think that we are Kings
Some see us as quite obscene
Some say we are royalty from Spain
A liar said from France
But never will a Romo abstain
To play a game of chance
Grandfather had a name like me
My father was a Savior
Those who know me will soon see
Whom this message is for

# Prose a Rose

Perhaps if prose smelled like a rose

It would be oh so fine
We would not need to seek in time
We would not need to seek to rhyme
All of our verse would then be kind

For if the poet did not know it
He would not need to suffer
The metered time would be a crime
And each verse would get tougher

For prose you see can quite freely
Be used instead of rhyme
And flowery pretensions
Would be the only intention
Of verse we find sublime

I speak of prose as if to pose

A riddle to the crowd
your thesaurus will soon be lost
and you will sing out loud

# Disney Land[1]

To Walt

We spend our lives looking for a Rainbow
With a pot of gold at the end
You can't eat gold, you can't love gold
We live in Disney Land
There is no admission, we are there
Fantastic visions and wonderful people
everywhere
We are prince and princess charming
Charmed I'm sure
This place called Disney Land is a wonderful life
Home is where the heart is and
We are Over the Rainbow
Why? Because we like you
So close your eyes
Click those Glass Slippers together and say
There is no place like home
When your eyes open you will be in Disney Land
With all of your best friends
And live happily ever after, forever

[1]pg 85

# Sunshine

Sad song, mad song Maybe just a glad song
That is why I'm writing this song

I love her, I need her Give anything to see her
She is why I want to live on

I think this, I think that No matter where I am at
My heart is like A beating gong

Someday I will kiss her Right now I just miss her
The dream that I cherish Will soon come along

The look of a god A smile or a nod
The flash of her eyes are like sunshine at dawn

# Thoughts

Catch the taste of something sweet
Catch the joy of dancing feet
See the flower whose scent surrounds
Like an antique merry-go-round

Please oh please let this happen to me
That my heart might come to see
Explosions of spring that never grows old
Losing the memory of winter's cruel cold

Remember the days of sweet delight
Into the ever starlit night
The soft sound of birds that fly all around
My feet feel like they never touch the ground

I miss my sweet love to share these things with
Her bright shining eyes like Beethoven's fifth
Perhaps I'll be with her inside a dream
And the light of my love will continue to beam

# The Reapers Wisdom

The kiss of death, temptations only friend
Simple device of my only spoken sin
Never say never unless you mean forever
For a promise made lightly is not my endeavor

The company of Princes and Captains and Kings
I know these things better as fanciful things
But Death sings lightly the sonata that might be
The horrors of resurrection are music to me

In the land of the living I will ever be giving
That temptress called Fate is most unforgiving
For no one listens to the prophecies of the wise
Most simple creatures would rather hear lies

The Witches of old knew these things better
But fetters of gold are still only fetters[2]

2 pg. 85

# The Tombstone Lament

Quietly rotting crow skulls
Sitting on a fence post
I can hear the monsters come
Looking out my window

Volcanoes like their lava hot
Somewhere in the distance
Wolves are howling at the moon
To better bother Mother Time
A train is screaming in my head
Filling me with thoughts I dread
Like a dog that smells
At fresh spilled blood
Showing teeth that rip the flesh
Eyes that twinkle very red
Let me stay tight in my bed

The death of winter screams in pain
As buzzards circle happily
Waiting for the dawn of death
Like butchers at the guillotine

Incessant screaming
At the gates of hell
The ferryman gambles
With your penny eyes
And demons whisper
Of their triumphs cheerfully
For heavens they have plundered
Very Mercilessly

No one knows the plight
Of the seventh son
He cries in the graveyard
When his heart is sore
Bones are rattling in their coffin
With a serpents burning fire
No time to give some incense
To feed the lonesome dead
Dead flowers have no scent
And they have no roots that feel

Tombstones die so slowly
When skies give up their blood
Little by little they speak more slowly

Of words imprisoned
In their face of stone

I pray there are no children
In the tombstone row
Only hidden faces on
The tombstone door

The crypts are very pretty
Lined up evenly
The reaper has his hands filled
Laying bricks of bone
He stacks them up to heaven
So we see heavens door
I'd like to have my ashes Sunk
On a boat at sea
But still I lament my tombstone
Which I shall never see

# Poppies

*for my brother John*

No one knows the poppies power
Til you've reached the seventh hour
One hour ago heaven was sold
For hellish fire in days of old

Dreams delight have now become pain
That tears you apart if you abstain
Once more you seek to have more pleasure
So intense that there is no measure

Your soul will seem lost in your endeavor
To see the things lost in your forever
The poppy looks so very pretty
But its scent surrounds you with no pity

Poppies seem simple poppies seem pure
Poppies cure things that have no cure
But one day you will reach the hour
You cannot resist the poppies power

# California

California it won't bore ya
That mythical place called California
Blondes, brunettes, and redheads oh my
Lovely ladies to make you sigh

Coppertone tans that smell so sweet
Lovely legs and lovely feet
Beautiful people that reach for the stars
Incredible restaurants, incredible bars

Fabulous visions of faraway places
Futurist places with mythical basis
We'll see California in fossilized time
The stories will never fade from our minds

These same silly things Atlanteans were told
When the earth was warm and knowledge was gold
And those events that bring us to the present
And drop us to our knees both King and peasant

We must be reminded of California's hidden treasure

The oceans, the mountains, resplendent without measure

Never again, will there be a place on this earth

Like the might of California's scenic golden worth

California it won't bore ya

## Memories

Nobody likes a quitter
Except when a beautiful lady
Quits saying no
Happily willingly Softly and passionately
Those things Beautiful memories
Are made of
Those transient Ever glow moments
That make life valuable
Memories of fresh beautiful Natural perfumes
That would sell for A million dollars an ounce
In department stores
These are the things We store in our Memorex recorders
That are gone when we die
Unless by artful cunning We can fix these desires into
Canvas paper bronze stone or
Any other messaging medium
To celebrate our prophesied Fifteen Minutes
But everything goes back to a celebration
Of the magic moment When that beautiful quitter
Said yes

# **Sweets**

I've seen the steamy jungle of death
I've steered the forbidden waste
I choose to choose the best things in life
And prefer not to choose in haste

Fine ladies make quite a collection
For many gentlemen of taste
But sweet wine is not at auction quite sought
Like a lady who somehow seems chaste

Holidays are meant for enchantment
When our hearts need be encased
The finest of times are found quite sublime
When two lovers have met face to face

Silly addictions we tease fearlessly
With never a drop to waste
Our hearts are still free to taste candy and thee
As long as no poison is laced

# Generation X

*For my daughter Katrina*

We are the ones called generation X
Drugs and guns and lots and lots of sex
Perhaps we'll die in just another sec
Party down cause it's just a train wreck

Living fast and gunning the run
Life is just for having fun
Never worry when the day is done
Never see the rising sun

Generation X has not a care
The previous generation had plenty to spare
The Emperor shall have no clothes to wear
For they shall laugh and shake their hair

Posers and Goths and Metal they seek
Perhaps cast off, but never a geek
If you see them you dare not peek
Or they'll drink your blood until next week

They are the product of a world gone mad
Some are wicked and some are sad
Surely this is not a passing fad
They are angry cause' The've been had

# Generation-X Revisited

They murder, they lie, they cheat and they steal
They don't know love and they cannot be healed
They know no Redemption cause' they feel no Affection
They have no faith in Heavenly Redemption

One Wonders, can they, really be that callous
To wonder to taste the drink from a chalice
Of life's Inconveniences, They find so unkind
The Incongruent workings of an Insane Mind

They like cut and paste, but that's the hard way
They spend so much time with the Dragons they slay
Their minds an open Book, giving' you dirty looks
Perhaps they wouldn't mind if they looked at that Book

No one really cares unless they're selling you Wares
And when you do the same they say that's not fair

They only think that Penance is the price of a bus

And when you speak of Evil, they will shout and cuss

You can't begin to learn if you do not pay attention

They think that Lust is a reason for Affection

Sum,. Es, Est., Sumus, Estes, Sunt

They think that they know, they think that they shouldn't

Life is a beach you Live and you Die

This is what they preach and they cannot cry

I'm thinking there must be, some place for this Ruin

A place on Uranus, but maybe I'm just foolin'

# Death

Quietly rotting corpses
Gathering all around
Giving up their dust
Unto the hallowed ground

Some souls will be lost in Hades
Memories lost in time
On oceans of earth
These things I am worth
I lose these things I call mine

The mortal coil slowly unwinds
Without admission of time
As rotting bones fall
To hear the last call
For nothing can I call mine

For Treasures unsold
I would give all my gold
I would love many ladies
Or possibly one
And would be quite undone
To lie here with no fun
In a world with no fear
Quietly rotting away here

If I could but smell
The flowers of hell
The flesh that decays
With sulpherous spray
A volcanic abyss
The torturous tryst
The demonic tension
I pray for abstention

But I think these things not
As I sit here and rot
In the bowels of the earth
I have proved what I am worth

# Maynard

For C.J.

I always wanted to be Maynard G. Krebs

But still I'd like Debs Who like Dobie Gillis

Who likes only blondes sometimes named Phyllis

We'd be at a beach a Clean and White beach

With surfing and surf

And those Debs would be fun

Out in the sun With hot dogs and buns

They'd call this place Malibu

The perfect human zoo

With wild teeny Shaking string bikinis

A Watusi in blue With Frankie and Annette

And all the Jet Set Under eighteen

And the evil Von Zipper Would torture and whip her

While Ward Cleaver drove by In a new red corvette

He hasn't paid for yet

And I'd go to San Francisco

To a coffee shop on north beach A real split the scene type place

And bang on my bongos Impressing the freaks

Cool Cat Daddy'o meets the malt shop
Where hairy dudes in turtlenecks and goatees
And Che Guevara type berets Sit and they talk
In a language they know That no one else knows
And I'd order espresso With nothing to go
From a waitress with black hair And horned rimmed black shades
And Mary Jane smokes
While poets converse
With bongos and slang On a stage made for rage
As page by page the poets would rage about drugs in the back room
They'd slam the door soon Cause junkies do fear
You looking in here
And Jerry Lewis would cry
When the bongos did die
But I'm Maynard G. Krebs
Who sees and likes Debs who like Dobie Gillis
Who sometimes likes Phyllis
And then I'll go forth on a three hour tour
In a seaworthy craft
And that ship will be crashed
And I'll never come back

# Treasure

Treasure your treasures
When they come as may be
Pick up your measures before they are free
Tickle your fancy as fancy is rare
Pay to the dancer the dancer is there

Merciful Marie she is quite absurd
Laughing and playing so she will be heard
She screams like a banshee when she comes to play
Pick up and stick up in one place she'll stay

I like to think of things seemingly precious
She wants to buy them up so she can impress us
The call of the wild it calls out to me
I fall in love so that we can be free

Treasure oh treasure quite bright and quite rare
When you find the X you are certainly there

## Fateful Fantasy

*For my daughter Kari*

What a sweet prize the eyes delights
Our children we tickle and play with
Such simple things we test what is right
To be the ones we are safe with

No horrid nightmares in between dreams
To trouble us in our play
No torrential boat fares to seize to be free
From all of the things we say

Sweet forest at sunset the skies in our eyes
Please set our inner child free
Our troubles are forfeit no pain in our souls
These things we will forever decree

And loves simple pain to be happy as one
No longer do we need to abstain
And one last question to seal our fate
That distant love that's never late

Please let us be friends in time
There is no punishment if there is
No crime

# When Angels Dream

For my mother

I once saw things through angel's dreams
Visions clear and not obscene
Bright blue sky and fluttery clouds
Where rivers flow and cool winds blow
Of all the things I thought I dreamt
The things I knew without contempt
I try to see these things again
I just don't mind I've changed my mind

*Please don't worry the celestial season*
*That brings us calm that brings us reason*
*Do angels think in heaven's time?*
*When angels dare to tread near here*
*Tethered to earth and bound to the stars*
*Tempered with the mercy of the fine divine*
*These simple things these unknown things*
*The things we sense when doorbells ring*

This house of cards the heartfelt rope
That ties us to our last hello
Our actor's lives are lost in time

That we perceive as Einstein time
Do angels think in ticking time?
I try to see these things again
Does heaven sing when angels dream?
Perhaps they dream of earthly things

Finis

# List of suggested reading

Alice in Wonderland and
Through the looking glass
The picture of Dorian Grey
Magick in theory and practice
Stranger in a strange land
Macbeth
A midsummer nights dream
Everything by Poe
Lord of the rings
The hobbit
Brave new world
1984
Island
The Electric Kool-Aid Acid test
Sometimes a great notion
One flew over the cuckoos nest
Fear and loathing in Las Vegas
Fight club
Clockwork orange
Twenty thousand leagues under the sea
The wizard of oz

Dune

The Bible

The Kama Sutra

The Koran

The Tao Te Ching

Siddhartha

Steppenwolf

"The Prince" by Machiavelli

The jungle

Animal farm

The odyssey

Sherlock Holmes

At least one book by dickens

A Spaniard in his own write

Conan - Robert e. Howard

H.P. Love craft

Edger rice Burroughs

Karl Marx

Jung

Freud

Jurassic park

Ray Bradbury

The seven voyages of Sinbad

e.e. cummings

Allen Ginsberg

William S. Burroughs

Samuel Taylor Coleridge

The book of lies

Frankenstein

Dracula

The invisible man

Dr. Jekyll and Mr. Hyde

Franz Bardon

Journey to the center of the earth

The time machine

And anything else you feel like reading.

But remember: "Reading after a certain time diverts the mind too much from its creative pursuits".

"Any man who reads too much and uses his own brain too little falls into lazy habits of thinking"

*Albert Einstein*

# Notes

1- I often am afraid that this poem would be interpreted as sarcasm, it is not. I grew up with Walt every Sunday on the T.V. and the Mickey Mouse club. I love Disneyland© and what I have simply stated is that Disneyland© is a microcosm of the best of the world that we have around us every day. Everyone should experience the Magic Kingdom.

My hope is that you return from there with the same appreciation for the world that you had at Disneyland©.

It should be noted that I do not wish to infringe upon Disney's copyright as I do not know how to take care of this problem I have called it Disney Land with a space. I hope I can get permission in the future. As that is how it is intended, note the ©'s above.

2- A fetter is a shackle something that holds you down

3- or Religion, since god is the crux of religion I have taken the liberty of misquoting.

# Art Credits

Page 15 Vivitrous by Leonardo da Vinci

Michelle's Art —My niece Michelle is a very talented artist. She did not do the works for the book but they just seemed to fit. The originals of some are in color and are very fantastic. She can be found on the internet as DarkSyren, or on My Space as Syren where you can see some of her work. Her works are found on pages 21, 22, 28, 32, 34, 37, 39, 40, 42, 46, 48, 52, 58, 64, 70, 73, 74, 78, 80, and, 92

My art- on page 18 is part of a work I did in Photoshop, Bryce 3d and Poser; I call it "stairway to heaven". On page 44 is "the genie" created with Photoshop. On page 60, 67 and 76 are photographs I did in Photoshop.

Katerina Koukiotis Art- she did the cover art and a small version on page 84. I colorized the cover and got an o.k. from Katerina. When I was trying to find a cover for the book I "googled" the words angel and dream then I went through many pages that were not what I wanted. Then I came to Katerina's drawing. It was perfect. I immediately emailed her for permission to use it. She gave me permission on the condition that I send her a copy of the book (note to self- if this book does anything show her you appreciate what she has done) . She does custom work and has posters for sale at the website at the beginning of the book. Interestingly enough the cover art was originally going to be a baby instead of an adult. I am so glad she changed her mind. I just love that drawing.

# The Fool

I am the fool
I crossed the abyss
A crocodile here a tiger there
As I step into the chasm of death
I had no fear

As the devil laughed and then he cried
Another soul lost to the higher cause

I am a fool
But still I live
To seek the higher gate
That only a fool can seek
These words that echo
Through the halls of time

Only the few will think things through
Many lives lost at precious cost
You that understand
Must simply follow direction
As directions go

Do it slow
And you will know
The law will be revealed
Only by a fool

www.ingramcontent.com/pod-product-compliance
Lightning Source LLC
Chambersburg PA
CBHW051708040426
42446CB00008B/779